Metaxis; Where You Can Find Me

poems by an immigrant

Annjanette C.

/ BookLeaf
Publishing
India | USA | UK

Made with ❤ on the BookLeaf Publishing Platform
www.bookleafpub.in
www.bookleafpub.com

Dedication

for the different versions of myself
i often think of,
for who i am now,
and for the ones
i have yet to become.

Preface

It's been more than three years since I last hugged my family. Since I packed my life into a few boxes, and left the house at Royal Meadows. The moment I took the first step onto the plane that changed everything.

I didn't know what waited for me—only that I had to keep going. There was no promise of what would become of me, only faith that the people I loved were still cheering me on from home.

Now, years later, I've built a life from the pieces I carried. I've met good people, found new light, and learned that belonging doesn't mean staying still.

I still don't know where I'm headed next—
but wherever I end up,
I know I'll find my way home.

Acknowledgements

I cannot believe that we're here—that I can finally hold a book I can call my own.
Like the journey that inspired it, I wouldn't be here without the people who carried me along the way.

To my loving husband—thank you for being my safe space. For allowing me to explore my creative energy without judgment, only love. I am endlessly grateful to have found a love as pure as yours.

To my parents, for believing in me—you both inspire me to become the daughter you can be proud of every day. To my siblings, who are each finding their own way in life, know that I'm always here whenever you need me.

To my support system—Ernie, Jessica and Starmajex, Melody and Alfonso, House Ewok—and to all those I've come to know here: thank you for making this journey bearable, for accepting me as I am, and for reminding me that kindness can cross oceans.

Thank you.

I never thought this small dream would come true, but it

did. Thank you for giving me the freedom and courage to share these years of my life with you. Whether I know you personally or not, if these pages have brought you even a little strength, compassion, or courage, I am forever grateful.

Until next time,
Jane

PART I: the leaving.
sixty-five pounds of life

65 lbs.
there's 65lbs of space available.
tell me how,
how does one fit themselves in there?

papers, passport, packages.
mom packs them heavy.
i see in her movement, the urgency,
the need to make sure i'm all set.
but in her eyes, i see fear.
i see sadness.
her firstborn's about to leave the nest-
with no guarantee when she'll see her again.

boxing up my room, whatever i don't need.
whatever fits, come with me.
picking apart myself:
which is necessary
for survival, for identity,
a sliver of me i can keep.
it was a wake -
of the things that made me whole.
whispering soft goodbyes.

in a few boxes,
most of me laid to rest.
the rest becoming restless as days pass by.

please tell me,
that in the small crevices in between my clothes,
i can bring my old book,
a trinket,
an old stuffed toy -
in 65lbs, maybe i can sneak a few,
pieces of the person i once knew.

2. look! it's a plane!

i would look at planes that flew by,
turn to my friends,
point up— "that's mine!"
japan, korea, los angeles?
anything is possible.
see how far it went,
until it's gone.
how big the world was,
for someone as young as me.

then at twenty-three,
home became scarce.
every smile,
every meal,
each second counted.
my heart dug its nails,
keeping me here–
grounded.
counting down the days,
i counted moments.
royal meadows dwindled.
NAIA grew closer.
the world began to spin.

my mind was stuck on repeat:
the kisses and good-byes.
i wasn't me anymore—
it was someone else
who needed to be the adult.
who had to be strong,
strong enough
to carry dreams,
responsibilities,
and herself.

i used to look up;
now i looked down—
down below as we flew.
watched while it was still there,
wondering if i could point,
which car carried the ones i love.
stopover at japan,
land in *LAX*.
answer with a smile—
a mantra of arrival.

look how far the *philippines* is.
how big can the world be?
anything was possible—
except staying.

3. borrowed tongue

we try to speak english as fluent as possible.
a point of pride within us.
intelligent-sounding,
corporate ready.
back home,
people would praise you.
they respect you more,
when you speak the language—
a borrowed one.

english was the first language i learned
before *tagalog*.
it was like a prophecy.
as if it was written—
one day,
it would be my weapon.
you hold back the natural roll of your tongue,
"three" instead of "*trree*".
we grew up believing
the accent is the enemy.

few days in,
people told me there was no accent—
no trace,

no remnant of home through my lips.
for a moment,
it felt like a praise.
but what if—
it was colonialism?
in a land where people came from everywhere,
who am i?
i correct myself when i sound "incorrect".
they barely bat an eye.
they listen to you,
not for where you came from.

i wonder,
through pauses
between words i can't remember—
will i be able to hold my tongue?
keep it as it is,
the way my mom spoke to me.
natural. known.

4. thingimabobs

a box of letters,
fragile,
careful around the creases –
in my mind,
like a roadmap to the past,
where words were fleeting,
and love was here.
Now it breathes
through this box
seemingly heavier.

instax photos
blurred by laughter,
of moments slipping past,
the flash freezing us
in a space of belonging.
hidden in my wallet
those with me,
who was always within reach.

a promise ring,
covenant that stood its ground.
talisman of strength,
that kept me believing.

wrapped on my finger—
heavy on my hands.
a reminder
of who i was fighting for.

an old shirt,
its fabric thin
i wear it to sleep.
it holds comfort—
witness to my rest.
when darkness falls,
i can pretend
that i'm in my room
and my sister
just a whisper away.

when my heart broke
i brought what would fit the cracks.
for now,
these are enough—
enough to keep me going.

5. in a split second

riding the bus
your hand meets the metal—
and in a split second,
you see
the inside of a jeepney.
then your hand taps the card,
and you walk on.

catch the sunset,
its golden reprise—
you close your eyes
and in a split second
you hear familiar laughter—
dad telling stories
over smoked tilapia,
chills down your spine.
you walk straight home.

the room again,
drawers full of dust,
as empty as my suitcase.
you eat dollar noodles—
and in a split second,
it's raining,

everyone home
eating the same.
now you're alone.
you finish it all.

an echo
reverberates gently
in a split second,
you wish you could pause—
and in that same split second,
your hand lets go.

6. so she stayed

they don't allow liquids in,
so she held
the tears i couldn't bring.
i see her unsettled,
unsure
of what awaits her.

only one plane ticket.
she begged to stay with me,
but the plane wouldn't fly—
her presence
too heavy.

left with her,
a promise:
i won't be long.
sit still,
with my tears.

she believed me.
and frankly,
i wish i did too—
that nothing would change
as long as she stayed.

so she did.
watched as planes came and went,
worn thin,
left wondering
where i was,
when,
and if i'd be back.

7. homesick in english

i talk to strangers with ease.
"how are you"
comes easier than hello.
when i explain,
i do it with ease—
no more lost words.

hearing myself,
it pains me
that i feel happy,
for i sound different.

but in the quiet,
the echo comes:
a gust of air,
a comfort—
remembering.

PART II: the surviving.

in the valley

in two months,
the trees have their moment.
i watch in awe as they shed—
it was my first fall
yet no one had to tell me,
i knew what was happening.

the streets i've come to know
shift with the season.
the air, cool and dry,
pumpkin spice in cups.
i take a sip.
fall,
just might be
my new favorite.

on fridays, tacos—
a treat after a long week.
i eat under a small lamp;
faint sirens outside.
i feel no fear.
nothing out of place.

two hours to downtown—
a chance for solitude
without being alone.
i watch people come and go
and wonder:
among thousands
in this bright city,
who shares this feeling
with me?

weeks pass,
no mistakes now—
no pauses for directions;
no consonants left clicking.
when i say home
without care,
just numbness—
it's the *san fernando valley*.

9. south oaks pointe

listing writes:
"one bedroom apartment"
hope flickers.
"$1800"
next.
"must have 650 credit score"
each one, harder to understand—
someone with nothing to her name
looking for something perfect.

along sepulveda,
i knock on doors,
call every number—
from "perfect"
to "just enough"
where numbers make sense.
maybe i can live anywhere,
so long as it can fit two.

every doorway a glimpse
of what life could be—
my love finally coming to me.
i believed, even without guarantee
that he'll be here

so i searched for one
that could shelter home.

listing writes:
"studio apartment"
simple enough.
"$1500"
it'll work—
if he comes.
when he comes.

when you walk in,
you see all the corners of the place.
one window,
just enough light in this hollow box.
chipped painting in cabinets,
the blinds not opening fully.
it wasn't perfect.
it was just enough.

i was given the key.
signed my very first lease.
one deep breath—
my own place,
at twenty-three,
a month's rent paid,
waiting for my love

to be here,
with me,
at home

10. versions

there once came a sister,
who answers crying calls at 1am.
she's tired—
spent,
yet she answers.
she has to.
why does she?

there once came a young adult,
who had to smile her way to survive.
cries in whispers,
bore witness to the dangers of the world,
and faces it anyway.
she needs to.
who's with her?

there once was a girl,
who had to hide to be safe.
the world, too cruel.
life alone, too quiet.
she wishes she never left.
hated the commute,
done with darkness taking over too early.
but she can't show herself.

each day she fades,
little by little.

i watched her chip away.
i continue to smile—
for everyone else,
i have to.

11. stable.

the phone rings.
"hello?
yes, how can i help you?"
i hope my smile is heard.
"let me ask—" *(when will this end?)*
"—and see how we can help."
lord knows i need it.

"the apartment? it's so fun living on my own!"
i'm eating food i've reheated three times now.
someone points at my plate.
"yeah, i made so much!"
the vinegar of the *adobo*,
sharper each time it's warmed.
"i can't believe how independent i am,"
and how easily it gets old.

later, i open the fridge.
cold air, quiet water.
my throat dry.
"i'm so thankful for the life i have,"
but still yearning
for the one i had.

the bed feels too big.
"i thank the lord for i am safe."
am i ungrateful?
"of course not."
i see the good.
just as i am now,
life is stale—

"stable."
i've wanted stable for months now.
"few more weeks before he comes."
finally.
maybe then,
i'll stop talking to myself.

12. dearest you

it wasn't easy for you to leave when you did.
for this, i see you.
you were strong enough to carry everyone's dreams with
you.
for this, i'm proud of you.

but you can't deny,
this isn't all it was.
i've seen you rewatch series
over and over again.
you knew it was better—
than silence.

you were so good
in convincing people
that living here is great.
but you knew what you were doing.
you would wish they'd come.
you hoped they'd know—
you were anywhere close.

i saw you hold your tongue.
you didn't want to admit it,
but i know the truth-

you felt relief
when it almost didn't work out.
but you felt embarrassed–
coming back
after making a big deal about leaving.

and you know,
all it takes is:
"it's okay, you tried.
come home"
you'd be on the first plane back.

but you let pride run the show.
you wanted to prove you can make it.
whatever it is, you could take it.
you are your mother's daughter.
and though they saw resilience,
courage,
i saw regret.

it hurts to know you.
they had you
believing this was purpose,
when all this
was a desperate attempt
to be someone
worthy of praise.

i wish you'd let us go home.
now we're in too deep.
i'm left to figure out
if this was for the best.
if only you can help me,
skip to the good part.
but you won't.
you prefer this *fucking* journey.

i don't have a choice.

13. what survived the mirror

mirror, mirror, on the wall—
enlighten me.
do i still look angry
when i explain?
no matter what i say,
i make sure my point gets through.

i move my hands when i talk,
even over the phone—
like i did in college.
small idiosyncrasies
still slip through the cracks.

mirror, mirror,
my eyes match my mother's—
more than ever.
my father's kindness
translates through my gaze.

my freckles multiply,
constellations
from every battle i've fought.
i trace them slowly.

mirror,
a witness to what changed
and what stayed.
the girl waiting for me
can still recognize my face.

mirror me more,
that i may know—
los angeles has not changed me entirely.
i still love the same,
if not,
more.

14. the sun loves california

the december air was harsh.
it taught me about puffers—
those that'd keep me warm.
but the sun loves california.
so even in these dark times,
it takes its chances.

the sun used to make my skin burn.
but now as i shiver,
it became a warm embrace—
fuels the light i keep steady,
in between my ribs.
i exhale around it,
hoping i radiate some.

my ribs work overtime,
shielding my light from my tears.
that even if floods and winds try,
it will never perish.
the embers of yesterday,
keep it fiery.

i thought the california sun
was losing its heat.

but maybe i've known
to burn
just as much from within.
it no longer hurts.
the california sun no longer scares me.

PART III: the homecoming.
the quiet art of belonging

the morning smells like his and hers shampoo.
the shower steam softening the mirror's scars—
of a time when I was alone,
a face that once waited.

the light turns green as anticipated,
my heart lingered a beat more.
i watch him cross
as seconds count down.
itake a deep breath.
i'll see him tonight.

i say hello to the bus driver—
not because i know her,
but because i want to.
a nod of thanks for the work she does.

the ride hums with the engine.
the woman beside me
closes her eyes,
a deep, deep breath–
we exhale the same.

on weekends,
we go to *Granada Hills*,
or maybe downtown,
spend time with newfound friends,
eat foods we've come to know.
laugh at inside jokes
we're here long enough to know.

at night,
we come home with joy—
greeted by our baby dog.
the streets soothe us to sleep.
the house,
finally,
becoming home.

16. keep it safe

i've changed so much, since then.
it terrified me—
the world wearing two faces.
but sometimes,
people find me:
those who make me remember
who i am.

i grew doubtful of others.
suspicious of their intent.
but i've learned to ask
to want to understand,
listening like it's a prayer.
i remember
who i can be for them.

i've carried light from where i'm from,
made of tropics, sun, and prayer–
never thinking i'd have to guard it.
yet the world kept adding stones
to the walls i've built,
to keep it safe.

still, i was made to feel—

to care, to love, to connect.
people saw my light,
i saw theirs.
nothing lasts forever—
i thought mine would
if i kept it.
but i'll never know if it can grow brighter,
unless i set it free.

17. namesake

my name once belonged
to the odd one out—
the girl who said yes before thinking.
now it means standing—
learning to live
not just for everyone,
but for herself.

my name once carried a young girl
who learned early
not everything comes easy.
now it feels like salvation—
a small beginning, again.

when someone says my name,
i return a quiet smile.
when they spell it out,
they often miss a letter or two,
but i'm not bothered anymore.
i know who i am.

my name keeps being written—
in forms, in lines, in waiting rooms,
said in class,

an introduction to who i am.
but who i am
lives beyond the ink,
still learning how to answer.

and in the quiet of night,
i don't have to say it.
for my name holds
all the seasons i've come to know.

i don't have to say it—
i know who i am.

18. for the ones who left

for the ones who had to put their dreams on hold,
to make way for the ones they love.
for the ones who cried alone,
so the ones back home wouldn't worry.
for the ones who had to learn
how to figure everything out
while figuring it out.

for the ones who lied their way
into believing everything's okay.
who saved leftovers
because saving meant surviving.
who sent money home when the dollar climbed,
and found ways to stretch what little they could give.

for the ones who reached out to old friends,
hoping to feel close again.
who found joy in grocery sales,
and guilt when treating themselves—
wishing those they love
could be here, too.

this is for us.
for the ones who left,

and survived.

we deserve to live.
no one is asking us to be more
than we are.
we don't need to have all the answers.
what we can give now—
is enough.

we are enough.

19. saltwater, memory and light

the sea used to be a curse.
thousands of miles away
from the *philippines*,
it kept me away.
but as i feel the waves crash onto my feet,
perhaps it was trying to bring me
pieces of home i forgot to bring.

i can't tell
if the salt comes from the ocean air
or from my tears.
but i don't mind both.
they carry parts of me i've come to know,
parts i can recall with ease.
the waves keep crashing,
like the rhythm of my pulse.
it brought to me proof
that if they can carry
a proof of my longing,
it can also bring me back home—
even for a moment.

i watch the light scatter

across the blanket of sea.
always moving,
yet very still.
it's where it needs to be.

the sea takes what it needs,
returns what it can.
as it should.
i am both
what left,
what remains,
and what will come.

20. home is where the heart is

on a random thursday,
i quiet the usual worries.
what once was doubt
is now plans for tomorrow.
i used to ask if all this was worth it,
but i see my dog sound asleep beside me.
how lucky, that he feels safest in our bed—
a fifty-dollar mattress, secondhand,
the only one i could afford,
tucking us in each night.

i hear laughter from the living room,
my husband and roommates—
it used to be just him and me,
but joy seems to invite company.
our home smells of baked bread,
and time finally lets me be myself.

my husband doesn't need maps anymore.
his hands know the turns by heart.
no pauses for directions,
only wanting to see more of this place.
the place no longer feels unfamiliar;

everything feels like home.

i barely ask for solitude,
for i found peace
in this bright city.

when i say home,
i mean the people i found,
the places i've seen,
and wherever we end up living.
softly, i can say–
it's *los angeles*.

21. metaxis

in quiet pauses,
i chase what life once was—
but see where it's led me,
and wait, softly, for what's next.

i feel most at home
in the place i've made my own.
a glimpse of that old room,
and a part of me
still roams it.

my heart aches the same
whether i long for tropical *palabok gata*,
or watch the sun kiss the desert sand.
it wasn't sadness after all—
it was just how home should feel.

i've come to find
the beauty of the in-between.
perhaps the journey
was never meant to end.

forever somewhere between
leaving and arriving,

befriending the unknown,
and becoming.

i bask in its silent melody.
it moves, yet stays still.
to recall without remorse,
map out a life,
and see the magic in the present.

and those who've felt the same
can rest easy—
you can find me
in the metaxis.